What's Inside

Strap
On
Those
Sticks

From mountain peaks to snow-covered valleys, there are almost as many ways to ski as there are types of terrain. Which one's your way?

Skiing can push your skills and physical abilities to the absolute limit. It can be a meditation for those who want to get away from the humdrum and enter into a beautiful relationship with nature. Ultimately it's fun: Time to spend with friends and family while enjoying all the thrills snow has to offer.

From shooting down alpine slopes to cross-country trekking through snow-shrouded forests, from off-trail exploration and adventure to somersaulting through the air off the lip of a steep jump, it's all here for you to discover...

Turn the page, and find out what it takes.

Extreme Sports

Part One

- Get Psyched
- 'Sno Fun Being Cold
- It's Your Turn!
- Rocket to the Bottom
- Solid Gold

Downhill

**You crave speed.
Bulleting downhill, snow
spraying in your face, a race
to the finish against your
buds. That's the joy of
downhill, or alpine, skiing.**

Get Psyched

You gaze up at the slopes from the base area, just itching to get out there. You can't wait to feel the wind rushing past your ears as you barrel down the alpine trails . . . but hold on. Read up on the latest info about downhill gear before making for that chairlift.

S kiing equipment and technology have made big strides in the last few years. You've got a lot of choices now. Here's what you need to know to select the gear that's just right for you.

STARTING OUT

If you're a beginner, renting boots and skis may be the best choice for you. You'll be able to try out a variety of equipment without spending beaucoup bucks.

DON'T KNOCK THESE BOOTS

Ready to lay down some cash? First on your list should be a good pair of boots. They exist to move energy from your body to your skis to give you the most control.

There are three types of boots. The easiest and cheapest boots are called rear-entry. They're simple to get on and off. Overlap and mid-entry (or central-entry) boots are a bit more expensive but allow for tighter ski control and can be fine-tuned for fit and performance. When buying boots, proper fit is the most important thing. A good fit should feel like a firm handshake. Give yourself time in the shop to walk around in each pair of boots for a while—or better yet, try out a demo pair for a day—and don't buy until you're absolutely satisfied with the fit and feel.

SKIS MADE EASY

Modern alpine skis are narrower at the waist, or middle, of the ski, to help you turn when you put pressure on the edge that's pressed into the snow. Today's most popular skis, called super-sidecut skis, have super-wide tips and tails. The most extreme skis of this type are called hourglass, or parabolic, skis.

If you're starting out on traditional skis, choose a length that is about equal to the distance between your shoulder and the floor.

As you become a better skier, you'll use longer skis. The longer your skis, the faster you'll go. If you're using hourglass or super-sidecut skis, you'll want to look for shorter skis. Generally, the more aggressively shaped, the shorter the ski should be—about 4 inches (10 cm) shorter than a traditional ski.

BOUND FOR GLORY

Ski bindings are designed for two things: to keep your boot attached to your ski and to release your boot in case of a serious fall. Bindings are critical for your safety. Have them adjusted and maintained with the help of a good ski shop mechanic.

POLE VAULT

There's not much you need to know about poles, except this: Put your fingers through the strap and hold the pole grip with the strap between your palm and the pole. That's it. To find the right-size pole for you, turn the pole upside down with the grip against the floor. Grab the tip. When your forearm is parallel to the floor, the pole is the right size for you.

'Sno Fun Being Cold

Skiing is a blast—except when you're cold and miserable. Here's how to stay warm and dry.

When you hit the slopes, you'll want to be wearing three layers: silk or synthetic thermal underwear (including fleece long johns), a polyester fleece inner layer that's soft and quick-drying, and a wind- and waterproof outer layer. This layer should be "breathable" as well as waterproof, so that you don't get too sweaty. Picking the right socks, gloves, goggles, and hat is critical for your comfort on the slopes. Don't wear too many pairs of socks or socks that are thick and lumpy. Look for a warm wool or synthetic blend. Get wraparound goggles with full UV protection and shatterproof lenses. They will protect your eyes from sun, wind, and snow—and sharp objects.

MUNCH TO MOVE

More than anything else, you'll burn up calories like crazy on the slopes. Before you ski, load up on carbohydrates, and don't be afraid to take in some sugar and fat. Look for fat-rich proteins like sausage sticks. Drink a lot of water, and stay away from caffeine—it will make you lose body fluid faster.

KNOW YOUR SNOW

Skiers may not have as many words as the Inuit to refer to different types of snow, but they're building quite a list. Next time someone says he skied in mashed potatoes, you'll know what he means.

BOILERPLATE (also BULLETPROOF): Thick ice.

CHAMPAGNE POWDER: Snow so light and dry it can't be packed into a snowball.

CHOCOLATE CHIPS: Rock clusters poking up out of the snow.

CHOWDER: Chopped-up powder.

CORDUROY: Shallow, closely-spaced parallel grooves in the snow made by grooming machines.

CORN: Melted and refrozen snow resulting in kernel-size ice chunks.

CRUST: A frozen layer covering softer snow.

HARDPACK: Compacted snow caused by repeated grooming or skiing.

ICE: Dangerous skiing conditions; clear and breakable.

MASHED POTATOES: Wet, heavy snow.

NEW ENGLAND ICE: Ice so transparent that grass can be seen through it.

PACKED POWDER: Light snow compacted by skier traffic or grooming.

POWDER: Light, ungroomed snow. In some areas, particularly the western U.S., powder can be a foot or more deep.

WIND PACKED: Snow packed by the movement of the wind.

It's Your Turn

It can take a while before you move from snowplowing down a mountain to making light, quick turns that get you to the bottom faster than the lift seemed to get you to the top. But be patient! You'll get there.

Beginning from Point A to Point Ski, here are some basics you need to know.

When you're just starting out, you should either take a few lessons from a certified instructor or give yourself some time and patiently teach yourself the basic skills. Good things to begin with are learning how to glide forward on the snow, turn around, and get yourself up after a fall.

First of all, let's get you in the proper stance. Your skis should be about six inches apart with each foot straight under your shoulders. Bend your knees and lean forward a little bit until you feel your shins pressing against the front of your boots. Try to keep your center of gravity over your boots.

GLIDING

Shuffle forward on the snow one foot at a time, keeping your skis flat and using the poles only for direction. Slide, slide, slide. Relax. Slide, slide, slide. Take it easy, and don't rush. Soon you'll be gliding like a pro.

TURNING

To turn around while standing still, begin by imagining your skis are the hands of a clock. You're facing toward twelve o'clock. Pivot one ski by lifting the tip and turning it to two o'clock. Keep the tail down while you do this. Put your ski down flat on the snow. Now pivot your other ski in the same way until your skis are parallel. Repeat to keep turning. Use your ski poles for balance. Once you're turned all the way around, try reversing direction until you're back where you started.

GETTING UP

When you fall, remember to go sideways so you hit the snow and not the skis. Keep your hands up and in front of you so you don't hurt your hands and arms. Once you're down, you're going to want to get up quickly. Roll onto your side or your back so that you can move your legs and get the skis untangled. If you're on a slope, make sure your skis are below you and at right angles to the fall line (the steepest, shortest, and fastest line down a slope). Scrunch your butt close to your skis and roll onto your knees. Push up with your poles or your hands, keeping your weight forward and angled uphill.

SMOOTH MOVES

Once you've got the basic moves down, you're ready to move on up. Try these moves for more fun and control.

THE SNOWPLOW: The snowplow (also called the wedge) can be used for stopping but also for turning—a move that on a downhill run gives you the best control. Point the tips of your skis toward each other and then shift your weight to one ski. Put your weight on the right ski to turn left and on the left ski to turn right. When you're finished turning, bring your two skis parallel to continue downhill.

THE PARALLEL: After some snowplow turning practice, you may be ready to try parallel turns, where your skis glide parallel through the entire turn. As you're moving down the slope, move more of your weight to the outside ski and push the tail slightly out while keeping light weight on your inside ski so that it's parallel to the outside ski.

WATCH OUT FOR THESE: One of three symbols is used to indicate a trail's difficulty level. Green circles are easiest, blue squares require intermediate skills, and black diamonds are for advanced skiers. Double black diamonds indicate the toughest runs. When you ski on a mountain you've never visited before, ski a slope that's a rung below your skiing level. An intermediate hill at the place you always ski might be a beginner hill at another mountain. Generally, the bigger the ski resort, the more difficult the trails.

Rocket to the Bottom

You're positioned in the gate, surveying the course below you. You feel the tension— it's you against the clock. You listen for that loud crack— the starting gun—and then suddenly, you're off! Welcome to alpine racing.

The basic point of alpine racing is to get from point A, the top of a course, to point B, the bottom, as fast as humanly possible. There are five events involved.

DOWNHILL

The downhill event is all about speed and guts. On the principle that the shortest distance between two points is a straight line, the typical downhill course has few turns. A long course, it usually features a mixture of jumps, a handful of challenging turns, and long stretches where competitors glide straight down. Here's where racers achieve the fastest speeds of all the competitive alpine racing events. The racer with the fastest time is the winner.

THE SLALOM

The slalom is the shortest course with many gates and turns. Racers have to zoom downhill, skiing between pairs of colored poles called gates. If a racer skis outside a pole instead of between a pair of poles, he or she is disqualified.

THE GIANT SLALOM

The giant slalom is a longer course with more turns. Like the slalom, it is a technical event. There's no room for mistakes.

THE SUPER G

The Super G (super grand slalom) is the longest course. Like downhill, it's a speed event.

THE ALPINE COMBINED

The alpine combined event combines the times from downhill and slalom. The judges add up the slalom and downhill times for each racer to determine a winner.

LEARN THE LINGO

Now that you're living life in the fast lane, talk what you know. Here's some of the lingo you'll hear on and off the slopes.

APRÈS-SKI: French for "after-skiing"—what you call hanging out after a day on the slopes.

BASE: The average depth of snow on a mountain.

BOMBER: A person who skis too fast or out of control.

BOMBING (also BOOMING or SCHUSSING): Going straight downhill at high speed.

BUNNY SLOPE: The most beginner of all the beginner hills.

BUTT-PLANT: Falling upon one's posterior, which is (almost) always good for a laugh.

CARVING: Making turns with the ski edges cutting into the hill.

CATCHING AIR: Going fast enough to have both skis off the snow.

CRUISING: Making a long run at a comfortable speed.

FALL LINE: The straightest and steepest line down any slope.

MILK RUN: The first run of the day.

MOGULS (also BUMPS): Mounds and lumps of snow—some natural and others created by skiers.

OFF-TRAIL: Areas that are ungroomed, unpatrolled, and usually unsafe.

PLANKER (also TWO-PLANKER): A skier, as opposed to a snowboarder.

SKI BUNNY: A novice skier.

YARD SALE (also FLEA MARKET): A fall that leaves skis and poles in various places on the mountainside.

WHITEOUT: Poor visibility due to a combination of fog and snow. Usually occurs at high altitudes.

Solid Gold

Being a skiing champion is not just about going fast. You've got to have that drive to push yourself to the limit each time you go out there, and you have to know you can beat your best time again and again.

Here are some of the folks who made it to the top of their game—and walked away victorious when they reached the bottom of the slope.

SARAH BILLMEIER

Paralympic gold medalist Sarah Billmeier lost her leg to cancer at age five. Three years later she learned to ski, and she's been a winner ever since. In the 2000 World Championships, Billmeier won three gold medals and one silver in alpine skiing, including the downhill, grand slalom, and Super G competitions. In her career, she has competed in three Paralympics and two World Championships, winning a total of 13 gold medals. Her first gold was won at the first Paralympics in 1992, when she was just 14. Talk about having a dream and never giving up!

PICABO STREET

Picabo Street has a winner's spirit. In the 1994 Winter Olympics at Lillehammer, Norway, she won a silver medal in the women's downhill. For the next two seasons she reigned as the first U.S. woman to win the downhill World Cup title. Then she had a bad accident, hurt her left knee, and had to have surgery to repair three torn ligaments. But Picabo was determined to compete at the 1998 Winter Olympics in Nagano, Japan, and got back on her skis. About a month before, while skiing in Sweden, Street hit a fence and was knocked out. But she showed up at Nagano anyway, ready to race. For the women's Super G race, Picabo used downhill skis, which are longer than skis used in slalom races. The longer, faster downhill skis made a difference—Picabo won by one hundredth of a second and took the Super G gold medal home from Nagano.

JEAN-CLAUDE KILLY

Gold medalist Jean-Claude Killy grew up skiing in the French village of Val d'Isère high in the Alps, where his father owned a ski shop. As a young boy, Jean-Claude skied on the roof of his house, and at school he went out to ski at lunch time. On February 17, 1968, Jean-Claude won the men's slalom at the Winter Olympic Games, in Grenoble, France, capturing his third alpine gold medal and becoming the second man after Toni Sailer to win gold medals in all three alpine events. (Back then there were only three alpine events—downhill, slalom, and giant slalom.) Controversy surrounded Jean-Claude's slalom win because the mountain was choked in fog. Although two other racers beat Jean-Claude's time, it was unclear whether they had passed through all the gates, which were almost invisible in the fog. Finally, Jean-Claude's closest competitor was disqualified for missing two gates, and Jean-Claude was awarded his third gold medal.

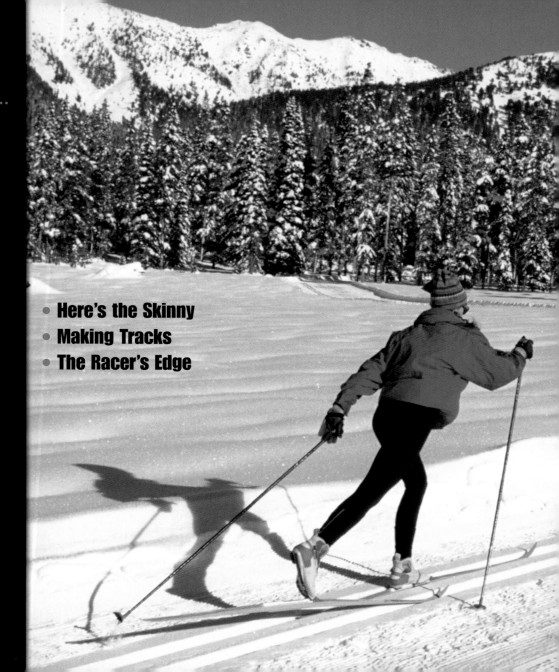

Extreme
Sports

Part 2

Cross-Country

- Here's the Skinny
- Making Tracks
- The Racer's Edge

Nature's your bag—
that and a good workout.
In the quiet hush that falls over the land—
the only noise the sound of your skis.
Get ready for skinny skiing.

Here's the Skinny

In Nordic, or cross-country, skiing, you're leaving your old pal gravity behind and turning to your own muscles to take up the slack. You move yourself across the flats and push your way up the hill. Bye-bye, ski lift; hello, workout.

Once you start out on the trail, it's not only exercise you'll be getting. The first thing you notice is that your skis are a lot thinner than alpine skis—no wonder cross-country skiing gets the name "skinny skiing." The woods around you will be filled with glorious views of snow-covered trees. You might even be lucky enough to spot some wildlife—cardinals, perhaps, or deer.

GETTING READY, GET SET. . .SKI!

Outfitting yourself for cross-country is both simpler and easier on your wallet than tricking out for alpine. "A reasonable budget? Yeah, I think I can handle that...."

BOOTS ON THE MOVE

Cross-country boots look a little like running shoes. They're lower cut, lighter, and more flexible than alpine boots. They're bound to the skis by a hinged toe piece that lets your heel move up and down and your feet flex. Most boots today have a hook or bar that snaps into the binding and can be released by pushing down on a release button at the front of the binding, usually with the tip of your ski pole.

THE SKINNY ON SKINNY SKIS

Cross-country skis are lighter and thinner than alpine skis. The newer all-fiberglass (or nonwax) skis have special patterns on the bottoms of the skis that grip the snow to help keep you from sliding backward when you're striding or skiing uphill. Before these skis came around, you had to use different waxes on the bottoms of your wooden or synthetic skis to get traction on the snow. Some people still swear by waxing.

Traditionally, you would use a cross-country ski ten inches longer than you are tall. Since the '90s, though, shorter skis have become popular, especially with those new to Nordic, because they're easier to start out on.

FROM POLE TO POLE

Poles for cross-country are lighter and longer than alpine poles because you use them to push yourself along. When you plant your pole in the snow, the handle should reach your armpit.

CROSS-COUNTRY, WARM AND COMFY

Cross-country clothing should be light, warm, and comfortable. Remember: You're going to be working up a sweat, so wear something that breathes and isn't too tight. If you wrap yourself up like a mummy, you're going to have a meltdown.

A good outfit would be warm pants or knee breeches, long socks, an undershirt under a button-up wool shirt or sweater, a light jacket, a hat, and gloves. If you're going to be out for a while, bring a small pack along and stuff it with water, extra socks and other clothing, and some food you can eat on the trail.

Making Tracks

You look out over the field before you, a sparkling expanse of fresh-fallen snow. But before you make your first strides across it, brush up on some basic techniques.

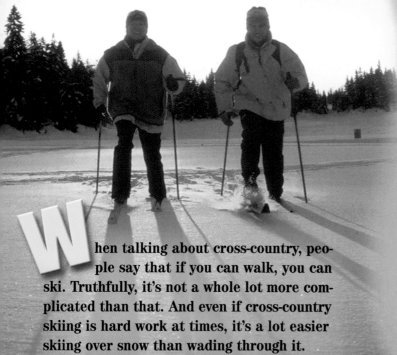

When talking about cross-country, people say that if you can walk, you can ski. Truthfully, it's not a whole lot more complicated than that. And even if cross-country skiing is hard work at times, it's a lot easier skiing over snow than wading through it.

GLIDING

First you need to learn how to glide forward. Start with a slow walk. Plant your left pole and glide forward on your right ski, pushing off from the pole. Slide your left ski forward at the same time as you bring your right arm up. Then shift your weight from the right ski to the left ski. Plant the right pole and slide forward on your left ski. As you glide on the left ski, start sliding your right ski forward and move your left arm up.

Start the sequence again. Step, push, and glide. When you have got this down, you're ready for double-pole pushing.

DOUBLE-POLE PUSHING

Keep your feet together. Plant both poles a little ahead of your feet, push down strongly on both poles, leaning forward. Push off as you glide forward. Now you're getting up to speed.

CLIMBING TECHNIQUES

(Use these for downhill, too.)

SIDESTEPPING: To sidestep up a hill, turn your skis so that they are at a right angle to the fall line. Step up with your uphill ski and put it down. Bring up your downhill ski and put it down parallel to the first. Repeat until you're where you want to be.

THE HERRINGBONE: Move the tips of your skis apart and keep the tails close together. (This makes a wedge, which keeps you from sliding backward.) Push up with your poles behind you, and walk up that slope.

MASTERING THE TERRAIN

In cross-country, most people start with track skiing, which is considered the easiest and most comfortable. A pair of parallel tracks is carved into the snow by a snowmobile. The snow is packed firm, so it's easy to put one ski in each track. Push off and glide. The tracks will help keep you stable.

BACKCOUNTRY AND OFF-TRAIL

When you're tired of the "easy stuff," you might want to head into the backcountry to ski off trail—make your own tracks. It requires more get-up-and-go, but it's a great way to enjoy the peace and quiet and beauty of the wild. You can ski through forests on old roads, or alongside a frozen stream. Set your own pace. Make your mark. But always bring a friend along. You don't want to be alone if you take a bad fall.

BUILDING STRENGTH

Get pumped! When you're ready for more speed and more of a workout, try the following techniques.

THE ADVANCED GLIDING STEP: If the basic gliding step is like walking on skis, then the advanced step is like running. To do it, push off or "kick" hard with the thrusting leg, keeping knees bent and weight forward, and give a powerful push off the pole as you take a large step and a long glide forward.

THE ADVANCED DOUBLE- POLE PUSH: The advanced double-pole push is another way to get your speed up on the flats and on descents. Like the regular double-pole push, you start with your feet level and your poles planted ahead of them. Now bend your upper body forward to put more pressure on the poles and push off strongly, following through with your arms. As you glide forward, keep your knees flexed. As your glide slows down, raise your body and bring your arms forward for the next pole-plant.

SKATING ON SKIS: When you're on a flat surface, you can accelerate by "skating" on your skis. It's basically just like ice skating or rollerblading, pushing off with one leg after the other. If you use shorter skis, higher boots with good ankle support, and longer poles, you'll move like the wind and get your heart and lungs going.

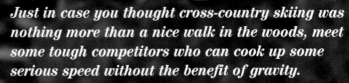

The Racer's Edge

Just in case you thought cross-country skiing was nothing more than a nice walk in the woods, meet some tough competitors who can cook up some serious speed without the benefit of gravity.

Cross-country racing requires speed, stamina, and strength. There are two kinds of races: classical races, which require traditional ski techniques, and freestyle races, which permit skating. Five separate events include individual racing, relays, biathlon, Nordic combined, and marathons. Race courses have a mix of flat, uphill, and downhill sections and are marked with flags, ribbons, and distance markers. These courses are designed to push the very limits of the racer's strength, skill, and tactical ability.

OLYMPIC MASTER
BJORN DAHLIE

In the 1998 Nagano Winter Olympic Games, Bjorn Dahlie of Norway won three gold medals for the 10-kilometer, 50-kilometer, and 4x10-kilometer relay, and one silver medal for the 15-kilometer. Dahlie has earned eight gold medals in his career, giving him the most of any single athlete in Winter Olympic history. With four silver medals to his credit, his overall total of twelve medals is also the highest. Dahlie trained by putting in more than 6,000 miles (9,656 km) a year skiing, cycling, canoeing, and hiking. What a guy!

BILL KOCH

In 1976, 20-year-old Bill Koch of Guilford, Vermont, won the silver medal in the 30-kilometer cross-country race at the Winter Olympic Games in Innsbruck, Austria. This was a huge moment in Olympic history. In an event usually dominated by skiers from Scandinavia and what was then the Soviet Union, Koch became the first American to stand on the awards podium. Despite suffering from exercise-induced asthma, Koch was confident during the race. "You push yourself to the limit, and then all you can do is try and hold on," he said. Today, up-and-comers train and compete in the Bill Koch Ski League, the Little League of Nordic skiing.

GUNDE SVAN

Gunde Svan of Sweden has six Olympic medals to his credit: four gold, one silver, and one bronze. At the 1988 Winter Olympics in Calgary, Canada, he was considered a favorite for all four men's events, but in both the 30-kilometer and 15-kilometer races, he underperformed, coming in tenth and twelfth place. For the relay race, however, Svan was back in the game. At each checkpoint his time was the fastest of the day, and when he passed off to his teammate, the Swedes were leading the Soviets by 27 seconds. In the end, his team won by 13 seconds. In the 50-kilometer race—the toughest race on the program —Svan again showed his true grit. Svan reached the halfway point more than a minute faster than everyone else. He came in first, taking the glory and the gold, and earning the respect of the spectators for his amazing comeback.

THE ULTIMATE JOURNEY

The Haute (High) Route is one of the most famous cross-country ski tours there is. It is roughly 75 miles (120 km) long and stretches between Argentiere in France and Saas Fee in Switzerland. Along this ultimate journey, you cross some of the highest and most beautiful peaks in the Alps. Much of the route is over glaciers and rough terrain, and there is the ever-present risk of falling into a crevasse or triggering an avalanche. There are no signposts, and the route must be navigated using Swiss maps and a compass. Experienced guides are a must. Before May, skiers generally don't even attempt to ski the Haute Route because the temperatures are too cold, and the weather and snow conditions are not optimal. Except for certain climbs where skis have to be carried, almost the whole journey can be undertaken on skis and finished in about a week.

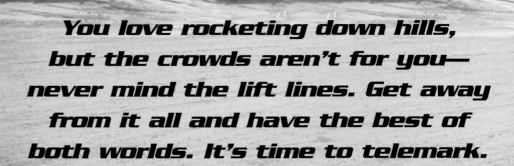

Extreme Sports

Part 3

Telemarking

You love rocketing down hills, but the crowds aren't for you—never mind the lift lines. Get away from it all and have the best of both worlds. It's time to telemark.

Telewhating?

What do you get when you cross alpine skiing with Nordic skiing? Telemarking, which has nothing to do with annoying phone calls.

Telemark combines the rush of speeding downhill with the go-anywhere freedom of freeheel skiing. Unlike traditional alpine bindings, telemark bindings allow the heel to lift, making it much easier to go up hills, even if it's a little trickier going down.

WHAT IT TAKES

Telemarking can be done on any cross-country gear, although many find it easier on telemark skis. A great thing about the telemark turn is its stability. It's almost like riding one long ski. You can use the telemark on all kinds of snow, but it really shines in soft snow and in powder.

WIDE SNOW BITERS

Originally, skiers would telemark using traditional cross-country boots and skis. But modern telemark equipment is more similar to traditional alpine ski gear. The fact is, if you are making turns down a steep slope, you'll need more stability on your skis to avoid falling forward, even when you've mastered the telemark technique. The skis are wider than cross-country "skinny skis," with metal edges that bite into the snow for greater control in the turns.

LOCK DOWN THOSE TOES

As in cross-country skiing, the binding secures only the toe to the ski, leaving the heel free to rise up off the ski. Often these are three-pin bindings, in which metal pins through a protruding toe lip center the boot in place and a hinged metal clamp clips over the toe to lock it down. This type of binding will lock your toe into your ski more securely than the lightweight cross-country bindings, giving you more control on your telemark turns. And you'll need it because the telemark turn requires you to

bend your knee deeply as you come around (see p. 33). The last thing you want is to have your foot popping out of the ski binding at that crucial moment.

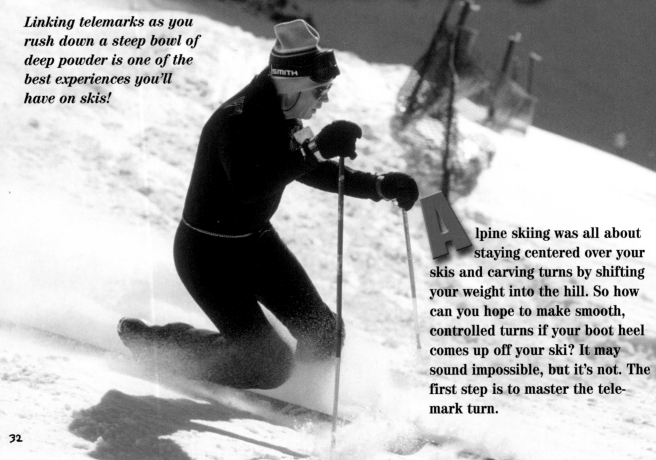

Freewheeling, Freeheeling

Linking telemarks as you rush down a steep bowl of deep powder is one of the best experiences you'll have on skis!

Alpine skiing was all about staying centered over your skis and carving turns by shifting your weight into the hill. So how can you hope to make smooth, controlled turns if your boot heel comes up off your ski? It may sound impossible, but it's not. The first step is to master the telemark turn.

THE TELEMARK TURN

In the telemark turn you get into a kind of kneeling position, leading with your outside ski and trailing your inside ski with that knee deeply bent and your rear heel raised. Keep your position erect. To stay in control, put more weight on your front ski by pushing your knee forward. You shouldn't be able to see the toe of your boot when you look down. Since your heels are free, your feet won't necessarily go where you point them. The answer? Practice, practice, practice.

LINKING TELEMARK TURNS

Once you've got the turn down, get yourself to the top of a slope and link telemark turns one after the other. Keep the moves from turn to turn rhythmical and smooth, like you're dancing down the snow. That's telemarking.

STEP TELEMARKING

If you're in really good shape and more than a little brave, you can manage really steep slopes and cruddy snow. In a step telemark, step the lead ski across the fall line to make a wedge shape, and then bring your back ski next to it. This will bring you to a full stop after you turn, which is good for staying in control on tough terrain.

JUMP TELEMARKING

In jump telemarking you lift your weight off the skis quickly and forcefully, so they come up off the snow and you can turn them while they're in the air. Both step and jump telemarking are difficult techniques requiring incredible strength on long descents, but they can be the only way to descend on difficult snow. And if you don't need to turn on rough terrain, the telemark position is a stable stance for riding over bumps and through dips.

FINE-TUNING TECHNIQUES

Once you master the telemark turn, try working on your form to make your turns even smoother. Work on keeping your knees parallel, as if you were alpine skiing. As you make your lead changes, your rear foot will still go back, but the rear knee can stay closer to your lead knee. If you can feel your shin against the tongue of your boot, you're getting it. Another tip for smoother skiing is to set up your turn sooner, by directing both the front and rear knee toward your next turn. This helps you turn without having to steer your skis so much. When you're ready to change your lead, roll your knees into the turn (as if you were alpine skiing), press down on the inside edge of your skis, and presto! You're right on top of the next turn sequence.

Making Its Mark

The telemark turn was born in the same snowy crucible that gave rise to cross-country skiing: Scandinavia. The winters are long in Scandinavia, with most of the countryside blanketed in snow from October to April. It's no surprise, then, that skis have been an essential mode of transportation there for thousands of years.

The 19th-century skier Sondre Norheim lived in Telemark in southwestern Norway. The area had many long and difficult trails. Today it is one of the most famous cross-country touring regions in the world. Here was where Norheim invented Nordic ski jumping in the 1840s and pioneered the telemark turn in the 1850s and 1860s. You're not considered a fully knowledgeable Nordic skier unless you have some telemarking techniques under your belt.

FREEHEELING LINGO

BACKCOUNTRY: Public wilderness areas that are not patrolled. Skiers are responsible for their own welfare.

SKINNING: Skiing uphill rather than taking a lift or walking without skis.

SKINS: A strip of natural or artificial material that sticks to the bottom of your ski for skiing uphill. Skins allow for smooth uphill movement but catch the snow and don't slip under reverse or downhill pressure.

SLOG: Mountaineering and backcountry skiing terminology referring to a long, slow, arduous hike uphill. Usually an endurance challenge with repetitive motion over large stretches of terrain.

SWITCHBACKING: Zigzagging uphill rather than going in a direct, steeper slog.

THREE-PIN BINDING: Old-fashioned backcountry binding in which three pins anchor the boot onto the ski.

TREE LINE: The area on a mountain where trees stop growing at high altitude and rugged and treeless terrain begins.

Extreme Skiing

- Ski Big (or not at all)
- Power Powder
- Warning: You're out of Bounds
- High and Dry
- Jump
- Need for Speed

Do you have nerves of steel and buckets of cash? Maybe it's time to take up extreme skiing.

Ski Big (or not at all)

So, you think you're a totally radical alpine skier. You've taken the best that the trails have to offer, and you still want more. If you're in the best shape of your life and have nerves of steel, maybe—just maybe—you're ready for the challenge of extreme skiing.

Flying off a cliff at breakneck speeds, skiing gullies and mountain faces far from packed slopes and trails, floating downhill through new fallen powder snow—that is skiing taken to the extreme.

DEEP INTO IT

Extreme skiing takes many forms, but one thing you can always count on is that you're going to encounter lots of deep, ungroomed snow, or powder. The whole point of extreme skiing, after all, is to get off the beaten track, as far away as you can from the trail maintenance equipment and bunny slopes.

But before you go charging off, be sure you know the basics of skiing in powder. Expect to ski in depths of several feet, past your knees and up to your hips. And while the ideal for every extreme skier is to find that perfect slope where no skier has ever gone before, under a clear, blue sky after a night of snow, the realities are a different story. Powder can be light or heavy, or it can be covered with a denser layer of windcrust. Perhaps other skiers have gotten there before you, criss-crossing the slope with their own tracks. Whatever the conditions, be prepared with the right gear.

Skiing in powder is different from skiing on firm snow. It's like riding on a soft cushion rather than a solid surface. You won't always see your skis, so you have to learn to ski by feel. And the deeper the powder, the more unpredictable and dangerous it gets. Shaped skis are the best for powder. They have wide tips and tails that help you float on the soft snow, and their shape and design make for easier turns.

FAT BOYS AND THEIR BUDDIES

There are a number of special powder skis. The widest of them are called fat boys, which are the best for beginning powder hounds. They offer more stability than narrow skis, and their width keeps them from sinking too deep into the snow. On fat boys, you fall less, which makes starting out on powder more fun and less tiring.

Another kind of powder ski is the wide-body ski. These are wider than conventional skis, but not as wide as fat boys. Wide-body skis are best for difficult powder, like crust and heavy snow. The trick here is to be ready for changing conditions. You might be skiing in above-the-knee powder one moment and into a bed of windcrust the next. You'll want the float-ability of wide skis, but you won't want to give up the control you get with narrower skis.

Cross skis combine the best qualities of wide-body and shaped skis but are wider in the middle. They have a softer camber, or central arch, which allows them to bend well in soft snow.

Power Powder

When you're starting either off trail or in powder snow, you should begin practicing your moves on short and wide intermediate slopes. The reason for a short slope is that if you get into trouble, the slope's not going to go on forever. And starting from the center of a wide slope gives you plenty of run-out to maneuver in.

When you hit the powder, remember that the main thing is to keep your center of gravity over your heels so that your weight is evenly distributed. Your arms should be wide open and higher than they are when you're skiing packed snow, and both knees should be rolled slightly uphill so that your skis are edged.

DOWN-UP-DOWN POWDER TURN

The most useful turn you can learn for powder skiing is the down-up-down turn. As you cross the slope in a shallow track, lower your hips so that your heels push into the snow. The tips of your skis will tilt up a bit. Plant your downhill pole and bounce up and off your heels, extending your legs and continuing in the same direction. Lower, plant, and bounce up again. Kick-turn 180 degrees and continue downing in the opposite direction across the slope.

DOWNHILL TURNS ACROSS THE FALL LINE

Start on the fall line of the slope and start sliding down. Hold one pole up vertically, lower your hips over your heels, then plant your other ski pole and push off your heels, as in the down-up-down move. But as you extend upwards, move around the pole, and your skis will turn in the same direction. End the turn pressing down on your heels. Now try turning to the opposite side.

STEEP SLOPES

Powder skiing down steep slopes is not only more of a rush than intermediate slopes, it's also a lot easier. Your skis go faster, making it easier to turn, and the powder prevents you from going too fast. If you can handle a moderate slope, you should have no problem on the bad-boy slopes.

PUNCHING THROUGH POWDER

This technique helps you get your skis out of the snow and is good for skiing in deep, heavy, or crusty snow. Punch through your turns with your arms and shoulders as you go downhill. As you bounce up off your heels, you punch and uppercut your outside arm out and up toward the downhill turn. Your hands and arms end up over your shoulders. This motion will keep your skis from getting sucked into the snow.

JET TURNS

The jet turn is good for deep powder and heavier wet snow because, as you turn, the tips of your skis come up and out of the powder. This breaks the bond between the skis and the snow and makes for easier turns. Since your ski tips shoot up, this turn also keeps the tips from digging into the snow and turning you into a snowman.

For the jet turn, push your skis forward into the turn. This will force you into a backward lean. To stay in control, come upright again over your skis by pulling up with your stomach muscles and pushing off your poles.

Once you get all this down, you can proudly call yourself a powder hound!

Warning: You're out of Bounds

Whenever you're skiing off-trail, you're skiing out of bounds, away from nearby ski patrols and the other comforts of the play-it-safe skier.

The golden rule is simple: Never, ever ski alone. Let people know where you're going and when they should expect you back. Find out beforehand from someone who knows whether the area you want to ski in is open to adventurers and whether the snow and weather conditions are safe.

GO WITH A PRO

Steep slopes or frozen or wet snow are extremely dangerous conditions, even for pros. If you can, go with a ski instructor or mountain guide who really knows the area and type of skiing you want to do.

PACK LIKE A PRO

Professional extreme skiing guides are equipped for every type of danger. Here are some of the items they bring along: a topographic map, a compass and altimeter (to measure altitude); emergency food and clothing; and something that can reflect a bright light so they can be seen by a rescue party if anyone gets lost or hurt. Other useful items include a cell phone and the number of the emergency rescue service and a GPS

(global positioning system), which can pinpoint the group's location anywhere in the world. If the area they are skiing has crevasses (deep clefts, or fissures, in a glacier), they would also carry ice axes, ropes, crampons (spikes that attach to ski boots), and harnesses.

AVALANCHE SURVIVAL

If there's any danger of an avalanche, wear a transponder, a device that will help rescuers find you if you're buried in the snow. If you're caught in an avalanche, try to ski to its edge. If you can't, jam your ski poles in the snow and hold on tight, or hang on to a rock or tree. If you're swept away, try to get rid of your skis and poles and anything else that could weigh you down. Swim along the surface of the snow. If you get buried, keep your mouth closed and try to push to the top, clearing a breathing space in front of you. If you can't get out, try to move as little as possible, conserving your energy and air. The only thing to do is wait for rescue.

CORNICES ARE NOT YOUR FRIEND

Watch out for cornices, huge curls of snow that form on ridges and cliff edges. They can weigh tons and can cause avalanches when they collapse. The break line of a cornice slants and can start far from the edge of the ridge or cliff, so if you see cracks in the snow near an edge, get back! And even if you can't see anything, be very, very careful.

High and Dry

You and your buddies are on top of the world. An open slope of fresh-fallen powder stretches below you, completely void of ski tracks. But where are the trail signs? The chairlifts? The other skiers? You've made it to extreme skiers' heaven, a slope where no skier has ever been before.

The crown jewel of extreme skiing is going to mountain peaks that have never before been skied—the higher, the steeper, the farther away the better. The only way to get up to places like this is to hoof it with your skis and poles on your back (mountaineer-skiing) or rent a helicopter to take you up. Both require rigorous training, a greater time commitment than your average weekend getaway to the slopes, and some serious bucks. But even if your wallet can't handle the price, it's still fun to dream.

THE ULTIMATE SLOPE

In 1970, Miura Yuichiro of Japan became the first man in history to ski down Mount Everest. He and a party of Sherpas and cameramen climbed to the top of Everest's South Col. His plan? To ski straight down the precipice at the bottom of the pass. Reaching speeds faster than 90 mph (150 kmph), Miura used a parachute brake and came to a stop on his belly just a few meters from the edge of the precipice.

The event was filmed for a documentary, *The Man Who Skied Down Everest,* which won an Oscar for best documentary in 1975.

PEAK PERFORMANCE

The lure of the challenge isn't lost on Laura Bakos. In September 2000, she climbed Cho Oyu, the world's sixth highest peak at 26,243 ft. (8,201 m) located on the Nepali-Tibetan border, and then skied down. Carrying her own gear, risking avalanches, and avoiding deep cracks in the mountainside called crevasses, she made the descent in two days to become the first woman ever to ski from a 25,600-ft. (8,000-m) peak.

THE BIGGEST AIR

In March 1999, "sick air" (extremest of the extreme) skier Jeff Holden of Stoney Creek, Ontario, used a helicopter to scout out one of the biggest jumps on record. Holden flew 150 feet off a cliff in Cordova, Alaska. That's like skiing out the window on a building's fifteenth floor! Fortunately Jeff knew his landing would be in a steep powder field, since he would be reaching a speed of over 60 mph (99.5 kph) on impact. He also knew how to land: skis first, then knees, butt and back. If you don't land in that order, "you'll blow your knees through your face," says Holden. He landed safely and skied away for another day of sick air. Needless to say, this is NOT recommended for any but the most experienced and capable skiers—and maybe not even those.

Jump!

*Swoop, leap, and fly…and hope
for a happy landing.*

Ski-jumping began in Norway
about a hundred years ago.
It's quite a dramatic sight to see a
skier fly off specially constructed
jumping towers and sail through the
air above the spectators.

Ski-jumping scores are based as much on style as the length of the jump. Jumps have to be carried off with power, boldness, and precision, while giving an impression of calmness, steadiness, and control. Unlike freestyle, ski jumping is the ultimate in form and control.

Every jump has five parts to it.

FIVE STEPS TO SUCCESS

1. THE IN-RUN: In the in-run, you crouch down into an egg-like aerodynamic position, with arms back to the sides of your body. Keep this position while gathering speed for the second step, the takeoff.

2. THE TAKEOFF: The takeoff will ultimately determine how long the jump is. Quickly stretch your legs and use your feet to push off and launch your body up and forward over the ski tips.

3. THE FLIGHT: During the flight you try to keep your body forward over the skis with the skis parallel and tipped up slightly to get more lift. This is how to ride the air, staying in complete control.

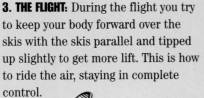

4. THE LANDING: You must land in the telemark position, with one ski in front of the other and knees flexed to absorb the impact of hitting the snow. The landing has to be soft and steady, and your hands are not allowed to touch the snow.

5. THE OUT-RUN: In the out-run, you have to straighten your body and come to a safe stop with skis together while keeping perfect balance.

If you're lucky enough to experience ski jumping, you'll learn what it really feels like to fly.

Need for Speed

You stand at the top of the starting ramp, a shoot that's nothing shy of 45 degrees steep. Adjust your helmet, grip your poles, and crouch down into your tuck. Are you ready for speed? You better be— you're about to go as fast as it's possible for people to go.

This is speed skiing, the ultimate velocity experience. The goal is simple: Go fast. Forget about turns. Speed skiers start on an ice-covered ramp and head straight down the mountain, aiming for speeds higher than 150 miles an hour (240 kmph), in 10 seconds or less. They get into a tuck, head and chest forward, knees and waist bent, elbows straddling the legs, poles extending behind. Warning: Don't try this on your own! Speed skiers require special training and super-special gear. Read on to learn more.

THE COURSE

You don't try to break speed-skiing records on any old mountainside. An uncontrolled free fall down a snow-covered slope is a bad idea. Instead, speed skiers use a specially constructed course, usually with three different parts. The first part, the acceleration area, stretches from 900–1,300 feet (300–400 m). This is the steepest and longest part of the course, often covered with ice, which the racer uses to pick up speed. The second part is the timing area, where the speed is clocked. The last part is the braking area. Here the slope usually levels off to a flat plain, so the speed skier can come to a safe stop. A typical speed-skiing run is over in a matter of seconds. Only ten officially sanctioned speed-skiing courses exist in the world, with three in the United States.

Still interested in giving it a try? One speed-skiing course is open to the public, in Snowmass, Colorado (part of the Aspen ski resort). For an extra fee you can take lessons and even enter in a beginner's competition.

THE PLAYERS

Besides Jeff Hamilton, pictured at left, other speed freaks have made their mark. Currently the world record holder is Harry Egger, of East Tyrol, Austria. He skied 154 mph (248 kmph) during the World Speed Skiing Championships in Les Arcs, France, in 1999. Women do it, too. Karine DuBouchet, of France, holds the women's record of 146 mph (229 kmph), also at Les Arcs in 1999.

Jeff Hamilton, U.S. Olympic speed skier, gets ready to take off (opposite). He was the first person to ski faster than 150 mph (240 kmph), when he broke the record at the speed-skiing World Championships in 1995.

THE GEAR

SKIS: Longer by 94" (about 240 cm) and heavier by 30 lbs (14 kg) than typical alpine skis, for maximum acceleration.

POLES: Bent to curve around the body to reduce wind resistance.

SPEED HELMET: Crucial for head protection in the event of falls. Speed helmets are fully enclosed, to protect eyes and face from the ice-cold wind. Aerodynamic, streamlined design also cuts wind resistance.

SPEED SUIT: Skintight for warmth and streamlining; made of rubber so that during a wipeout, the skier will slide instead of tumble. This helps keep injuries to a minimum.

FARINGS: These are wing like attachments to the boots, which direct the wind easily past the skier's legs. These are custom-made, usually from Styrofoam or a similar material.

Extreme
Sports

Part 5

The Big Three
Mogul Mania
Acro & Aerials

Freestyle

Get wacky. Get wild. Express yourself. Freestyle skiing, once known as hotdogging, became popular in America in the late 60s and early 70s. In the beginning, freestyle skiing meant "anything goes." Skiers pulled moves from skating, ballet, and gymnastics and combined them however they wanted. It was all about freedom. Today, freestyle skiing is broken up into three categories: mogul skiing, acro skiing (formerly called ballet), and aerials. Let yourself get funky and free.

The Big Three

Know your stuff before you flip, flop, and fly.

For each type of freestyle skiing, there are different ski needs. Mogul skiers can use regular skis and boots but prefer skis that are more flexible, with deeper sidecuts in the center for tight control. Some mogul skiers say shorter skis are easier for fast turns. Acro skiers use short, light skis that turn and spin easily when they're flat on the snow. Acro skis are stronger than traditional skis, have only a slight camber, or arch, in the middle, and turn up slightly at the tail. Acro ski boots are light and flexible. Aerial skis need to be as light as possible. Since all of the action takes place in the air, the ski's main job is to get you to the takeoff ramp and help you land.

GETTING STARTED

Although acro skiing is the least dangerous of the three types of freestyle—and certainly less risky than extreme skiing—for all three kinds of freestyle you will need to be in excellent shape and have already mastered all the basic downhill and cross-country skiing techniques. Coming to freestyle without this knowledge under your belt is like flying before you can walk.

One thing that's important to know is how to ski on your uphill ski, which will help develop independent leg movements. You're used to shifting your weight to your downhill ski, a basic technique of alpine skiing. Now see what happens when you transfer some of that weight to your uphill ski. For acro skiing, one should know how to do crossovers (the skis are lifted and stepped over each other), snowplowing backward, and kick turning (turning 180 degrees).

The moves for mogul skiing are similar to the ones needed for cross-country except that the mogul skier's legs need to be able to handle a lot more impact to keep the skis in contact with the snow.

Aerial skiers are advised to have some background in acrobatics, gymnastics, and ski jumping. Aerial skiers who want to somersault competitively are required to have a certificate from a qualified freestyle coach or judge. If you're unprepared, you ski at your own peril.

Aerial skiers

Mogul skiers

Acro skiers

Mogul Mania

Fasten your bindings—it's going to be a bumpy ride.

Moguls are bumps or mounds made when skiers carve the same turns in the snow. On each turn their skis kick up a little mound of snow, and after many skiers go by, the mounds grow bigger and become moguls.

The aim in mogul skiing is to turn as often as possible while keeping tight control at high speeds. Competitors are also required to perform two jumps on their bumpy race down the slope. In the early days of mogul skiing, there were no set rules, and amazing recoveries from spills on the snow were part of the thrill for spectators. Now, competitors are penalized for falls.

You need great physical strength, technique, and lightning-quick reactions as well as a sense of showmanship. Every mogul skier has a personal style—there's no business like snow business.

SKIING THE HOLLOWS, SKIING THE BUMPS

There are two ways to attack a mogul field. The first way is called skiing the hollows. You can stay in the dips and turns between the bumps instead of going over the bumps. The other way is skiing the bumps, where you ski over the moguls, turning at the top of each.

THE ABSORPTION-EXTENSION TURN

The most basic turn used in mogul skiing is the absorption-extension turn, where you bend your legs as you hit the top of a mogul, lean your knees into the turn, and rotate your skis into the new direction. At the top of a mogul, only the center of your ski is touching the snow. With so little resistance, it's an easy matter to pivot your skis.

THE JET TURN

Another turn is a modified jet turn (see p. 41). It's used for turning on larger moguls and at high speed.

JUMPING FROM MOGUL TO MOGUL

A crucial technique to learn is how to jump from mogul to mogul. You go off the top of a mogul at high speed, turn your skis in midair, and land on the next mogul. You need really strong legs and great timing to do this.

Acros & Aerials

Tricks, stunts, jumps, and flips add up to adrenaline-pumping action.

Both acro and aerial skiing involve tricky moves, but acro skiing can be more forgiving of mistakes. A wrong move off an aerial jump could cost you your life.

FREESTYLE SKI DANCING

Acro skiing is a combination of tricks and stunts transformed into a smooth, choreographed routine, performed on gentle slopes with dry, packed snow. Low on speed, perhaps, but way high on technique. You're judged on skill, originality, and overall perfection.

LEARN TO TURN—ON ONE SKI

Two popular turns are the royal christie (butterfly) and the outrigger. In the royal christie the outside leg is extended behind the skier, and in the outrigger the outside leg is extended to the side with the inside leg flexed.

TIP ROLLS

Plant your poles, jump in the air, and pivot 180 or 360 degrees around the ski tips. Tip rolls can lead into crossovers, spins, and jumps.

SOMERSAULTS

Rolls and somersaults require the most gymnastic skill and training. They involve headstands and handstands as well as forward and backward somersaults. In the front pole-flip, one of the most difficult tricks, you plant your poles in front of you, jump up, and somersault over your poles. Watch your wrists!

AERIALS—HOT MOVES IN MIDAIR

Aerial skiing—the biggest rush . . .and the most danger. Like mogul skiing, there were no set rules in the beginning. But after two skiers were paralyzed in 1973, rules were introduced to prevent the wilder skiers from going out of control and injuring themselves. The freestyle jumps are carefully constructed, and the judges look for perfect rather than daring routines.

There are two kinds of ramps designed for aerial freestyle. The floater ramp is horizontal and almost straight and is designed for upright jumps. A kicker is designed for somersaults. It's a steep, smooth curve built to throw the skier higher in the air.

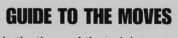

GUIDE TO THE MOVES

If you've put in the time and the training, you may be ready to grab some air with these far-out tricks.

THE SPREAD EAGLE: As you launch off the floater, throw your arms out to the side above your head and stretch your legs out to the side as far as possible. Now you're flying. Enjoy the rush, but don't forget to bring your legs back together right before you land, or you'll go from spread eagle to dead eagle.

THE DAFFY: As you zip off the floater, stretch your legs apart diagonally, so one ski points up and one points down. If you do this, you're definitely "daffy."

THE BACKSCRATCHER: Pop off the tip of the floater, tuck your legs up behind you, and throw your arms up and backward. Your ski tips should be pointing straight down, with the tails up behind your shoulders. After you "scratch your back," land with your skis flat on the snow.

THE HELICOPTER: This is an upright, rotational jump. After a good takeoff, you turn 360 degrees in midair, keeping your skis horizontal and parallel. Experts can do double or triple helicopters.

SOMERSAULTS: Inverted aerials are the toughest of all the tricks that use the kicker ramp and must be learned from a professional coach. You can somersault forward or backward in the air, with or without a twist. These are the coolest moves, but if you don't know what you're doing, they can be lethal . . .so get help, dude.

You're ready for action, and you can't wait to get out there. But skiing is more than just having fun—you have a responsibility to yourself and others to do it safely and wisely. Be a safe and savvy skier and you'll have the time of your life!

Ski Smarts

Skiing is a blast—there's no doubt about it. You love the scenery, the sense of movement and grace, the thrills. And let's face it—part of the fun is doing something you know is risky. It's up to you to be smart about the risks.

You want to ski safely, in areas that feel right for your ability, and you want to stay in control. If you don't, you can put yourself in danger. More than that, you can also endanger others. Here's a quick course on skiing dos and don'ts, safety tips, mountain etiquette, and everything else you'll need to know to make your skiing safe and happy.

KNOW THYSELF

Everyone on a slope hates a skier that's out of control. You're trying to concentrate, working on your turns and your form, and yet you fear for your life because there's someone right behind you who is skiing way too fast and falling all over the place. Remember:

- Ski within your ability, and stay away from trails that you know are too difficult.
- Don't ski faster than you feel comfortable.
- Know how to stop and avoid other people and objects, such as rocks and trees.
- If you feel yourself losing control, come to a stop and regroup.
- If you find yourself on a trail that's too difficult for your ability, look for an exit to an easier trail. If there isn't one, proceed slowly—sidestep down, snowplow, or if you have to, take off your skis and walk down.

MOUNTAIN ETIQUETTE

The rule is that skiers below you or in front of you have the right of way. They can't see you, so it's your responsibility to avoid them. If you want to pass them, be sure they know you are there before you move forward. It's also important to be aware of skiers behind you, even if you have the right of way. Don't block trails or stop where you can't be seen from above. If you fall down, get up and start moving again. If you need to stop to adjust clothing, put on your skis, or wait for your skiing buddy to catch up with you, move to the side of the trail. Also, whenever you merge into a trail, look uphill and behind you. Yield to other skiers.

SIGNS ARE GOOD

Always go skiing with a trail map, and pay close attention to trail markers and labels. Also note warnings for ice, rocks, and other conditions, and obey signs that indicate areas or trails are closed. Never ski beyond the area boundary.

CHECK THAT GEAR!

Make absolutely sure that your skis have retention devices on them to keep them from sliding down the mountain if they come off. A loose ski gains speed as it slides away, posing a real danger to skiers below. Check that your bindings are secure—not too tight and not too loose. Always check that your poles are attached to your wrists before you take off. And if conditions are bad, be sure your goggles give you enough visibility to see where you're going.

Conditioning

Take a deep breath. There's something about the cold air up here that makes you feel healthy and fit all through your body.

Skiing is more strenuous than you might think, given that you spend the day going downhill and then getting into a chairlift to get back to the top of the mountain again. The fact is, you're moving your body at all times, and your legs are getting the workout of their lives. Plus, your body's working overtime to make sure you stay warm and energized in this cold, high-altitude environment. Find out what it takes to be in the best shape for skiing.

FIT TO SKI

To be in the best possible shape you can be for skiing, you want to increase your aerobic capacity, strength, and flexibility. There are lots of ways to get in shape, including doing aerobic exercises, running, power walking, swimming, bicycling, rock climbing, and playing handball or golf.

Two of the best ways to get your body and mind prepared for skiing are kayaking and in-line skating. Both of these sports improve your dynamic motion skills and require the same kind of control you need on the slopes.

Whatever you do, make sure you work out on a regular schedule, at least three times a week, and for a minimum of 20 minutes per workout. It's also important to stretch before and after exercising (whether a day on the water or a day on the slopes) until you've gotten your muscles nice and loose. This will help your flexibility and balance.

SKI-SPECIFIC EXERCISES

GETTING UP: Sit on the floor in the corner of a room with your legs tucked under you. Push yourself upright with your legs, using your arms to support yourself against both walls. On the slopes your ski poles take the place of the walls. This is the best way to get up when you fall.

PUSHUPS: These build arm strength and help you use your poles more effectively. When doing pushups, keep your back straight and your body rigid.

UPPER BODY ROTATION: Stand with your hands on your hips and swing your upper body slowly around in a wide circle, first one way and then the other. This is important for performing turning maneuvers.

WALL SITTING: Put your feet flat on the floor and sit with your back flat against a wall and your thighs parallel to the ground. This builds up strength in your leg muscles, which will help keep your legs flexed while you are skiing.

Resources

ADDITIONAL INFORMATION ON SKIING

BOOKS

Where to Ski and Snowboard 2001
by Chris Gill and Dave Watts
Bath, UK: NortonWood Publishing, 2000

The New Guide to Skiing: A Step-by-Step Guide in Color,
Revised Edition
by Martin Heckelman
New York, NY: W.W. Norton & Company, 1995

Allen and Mike's Really Cool Backcountry Ski Book: Traveling and
Camping Skills for a Winter Environment
by Allen O'Bannon and Mike Clelland
Evergreen, CO: Chockstone Press, 1996

The All-Mountain Skier: The Way to Expert Skiing
Mark Elling, R. Mark Elling, Brian Elling
New York, NY: McGraw-Hill Professional Publishing, 1997

WEB SITES

Here are some Web sites you can check out to find general information on skiing, ski tour groups, and weather forecasts:

Weather forecasts: www.intellicast.com
Cross Country Skier (magazine):
www.crosscountryskier.com
National Ski Patrol: www.skipatrol.org
SkiCentral: www.skicentral.com
SkiNet (Skiing and Ski magazines): www.skinet.com
Ski Tour Operators Association: www.skitops.com
Snow Country (magazine): www.snowcountry.com
U.S. Ski Team: www.usskiteam.com

ABOUT THE AUTHOR

Pamela Pollack has had extensive experience in developing best-selling juvenile titles for such companies as Simon & Schuster and William Morrow. She edited and compiled *The Random House Book of Humor for Children* and wrote three titles based on the *Malcolm in the Middle* TV series, among numerous other fiction and non-fiction writing credits. She has contributed hundreds of reviews and feature articles to *School Library Journal*. Pam lives in New York City.

ABOUT THE CONSULTANT

Ron Leighton is an expert amateur freestyle skier who has been skiing since he could walk—maybe before. He has skied from the French Alps to the Colorado Rockies, both for personal enjoyment and as a representative of corporations in charity races. He is a resident of Hoboken, New Jersey.

PHOTO CREDITS

Library of Congress Cataloging-in-Publication Data
Pollack, Pamela.
Ski! / by Pamela Pollack.
p. cm. — (Extreme sports)
ISBN 0-7922-6738-9 (pbk.)
1. Skis and skiing—Juvenile literature. I. Title.
II. Extreme sports (Washington, D.C.)
GV854.315 .P65 2001   796.93—dc21   2001054445

Design and Editorial: Jack&Bill/Bill SMITH STUDIO Inc. Cover and series design: Joy Masoff.